Hello, Beautiful!

Desert Animals

WORLD
BOOK

www.worldbook.com

World Book, Inc.
180 North LaSalle Street, Suite 900
Chicago, Illinois 60601
USA

For information about other World Book publications, visit our website at www.worldbook.com or call 1-800-WORLDBK (967-5325).

For information about sales to schools and libraries, call 1-800-975-3250 (United States), or 1-800-837-5365 (Canada).

Library of Congress Cataloging-in-Publication Data for this volume has been applied for.

Hello, Beautiful!
ISBN: 978-0-7166-3567-3 (set, hc.)

Desert Animals
ISBN: 978-0-7166-3570-3 (hc.)

Also available as:
ISBN: 978-0-7166-3580-2 (e-book)

Printed in China by Shenzhen Wing King Tong Paper Products Co., Ltd., Shenzhen, Guangdong
1st printing July 2018

Photographic credits:

Cover: © iStockphoto, © Shutterstock.

© iStockphoto 29; © Shutterstock 4-28.

Staff

Writer: Shawn Brennan

Executive Committee

President
Jim O'Rourke

Vice President and
Editor in Chief
Paul A. Kobasa

Vice President, Finance
Donald D. Keller

Vice President, Marketing
Jean Lin

Vice President,
International Sales
Maksim Rutenberg

Vice President, Technology
Jason Dole

Director, Human Resources
Bev Ecker

Editorial

Director, New Print
Tom Evans

Managing Editor, New Print
Jeff De La Rosa

Senior Editor, New Print
Shawn Brennan

Editor, New Print
Grace Guibert

Librarian
S. Thomas Richardson

Manager, Contracts &
Compliance (Rights &
Permissions)
Loranne K. Shields

Manager, Indexing Services
David Pofelski

Digital

Director, Digital Content
Development
Emily Kline

Director, Digital Product
Development
Erika Meller

Manager, Digital Products
Jonathan Wills

Graphics and Design

Senior Art Director
Tom Evans

Senior Visual
Communications Designer
Melanie Bender

Media Researcher
Rosalia Bledsoe

**Manufacturing/
Production**

Manufacturing Manager
Anne Fritzinger

Proofreader
Nathalie Strassheim

Contents

Introduction

Welcome to "Hello, Beautiful!" picture books!

This book is about animals that live in deserts. Each book in the "Hello, Beautiful!" series uses large, colorful photographs and a few words to describe our world to children who are not yet reading on their own or are beginning to learn to read. For the benefit of both grown-up and child readers, a picture key is included in the back of the volume to describe each photograph and specific type of animal in more detail.

"Hello, Beautiful!" books can help pre-readers and starting readers get into the habit of having fun with books and learning from them, too. With pre-readers, a grown-up reader (parent, grandparent, librarian, teacher, older brother or sister) can point to the words on each page as he or she speaks them aloud to help the listening child associate the concept of text with the object or idea it describes.

Large, colorful photographs give pre-readers plenty to see while they listen to the reader. If no reader is available, pre-readers can "read" on their own, turning the pages of the book and speaking their own stories about what they see. For new readers, the photographs provide visual hints about the words on the page. Often, these words describe the specific type of animal shown. This animal may not be representative of all species, or types, of that animal.

This book displays some of the many kinds of animals that live in deserts around the world. Help inspire respect and care for these important and beautiful animals by sharing this "Hello, Beautiful!" book with a child soon.

Camel

Hello, beautiful camel!

You are a dromedary. You have one hump on your back. Some of your camel cousins have two.

two

You can walk for miles and miles. Sometimes you do not eat or drink for days.

one

Coyote

Hello, beautiful coyote!

You have large, pointed ears and a bushy tail. You look like some pet dogs.

We can hear your scary howl in the desert at night.

8

Gerbil

Hello, beautiful gerbil!

You are a Mongolian gerbil.
You have long back legs and
a long, hairy tail.

You like to be with other
gerbils. You live in holes
you dig in the ground.

Hare

Hello, beautiful hare!

You are a jack rabbit. You have long ears, big eyes, and a short tail. But you are not really a rabbit!

You use your strong back legs to l e a p across the desert.

Hyena

Hello, beautiful hyena!

You are a striped hyena. Your strange howl sounds like a person laughing!

You are a good hunter. Sometimes you find dead animals to eat. You have powerful jaws and strong teeth.

Lizard

Hello, beautiful lizard!

You are a Gila monster. You bite! We will not get close to you.

You keep fat in your belly and thick tail.

You use this fat for food when there is nothing to eat.

Owl

Hello, beautiful owl!

You are a burrowing owl.
You nest in holes dug by
other animals.

You are a **brown** and
white owl with long legs.

Coo-whooh! Coo-whooh! is
the sound you make.

Rattlesnake

Hello, beautiful rattlesnake!

You are a western diamondback rattlesnake. You have a rattle at the end of your tail.

You shake your rattle to warn other animals to stay away! A bite from you hurts badly!

Scorpion

Hello, beautiful scorpion!

You are a stripe-tailed scorpion. You have eight legs and a lot of eyes!

You catch animals to eat with your large claws. Sometimes you sting other animals with the end of your curly tail.

Tarantula

Hello, beautiful tarantula!

You are an Arizona blond tarantula. You are a big spider with eight hairy legs.

When you rub your back legs, you throw tiny, pointed hairs into the air! Ouch!

Vulture

Hello, beautiful vulture!

You are a griffon vulture. You use your wide wings to fly high in the air.

Your sharp
eyes spot dead
animals to eat.

Wren

Hello, beautiful wren!

You are a cactus wren. You make your nest in prickly cactuses.

There are **black** spots on your back, wings, and tail feathers. You are a noisy bird!

29

Picture Key

Learn more about these desert animals! Use the picture keys below to learn where each animal lives, how big it grows, and its favorite foods!

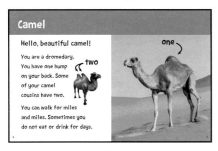

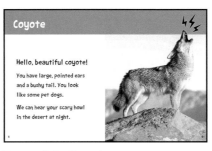

Pages 6-7 Camel
The dromedary *(DROM uh dehr ee)* is also called the Arabian camel. It lives in dry parts of India, the Middle East, Africa, and Australia. It grows up to 7 feet (2 meters) tall. People in the desert feed their dromedaries dates, grass, and such grains as wheat and oats. But when food becomes scarce, a dromedary will eat almost anything.

Pages 8-9 Coyote
Coyotes *(KY ohts* or *ky OH teez)* live in the United States, Canada, Mexico, and parts of Central America. An adult coyote measures about 3 to 4 ½ feet (1 to 1.4 meters) long, including its 11- to 16-inch (28- to 41-centimeter) tail. It stands about 1 ½ to 2 feet (0.5 to 0.6 meters) high and weighs from 15 to 50 pounds (7 to 23 kilograms). Coyotes chiefly eat rabbits and rodents. They also prey on antelope, deer, goats, sheep, and the pets of urban residents. Coyotes also eat insects, small birds, reptiles, animal remains, fruits, and mesquite beans.

Pages 10-11 Gerbil
The Mongolian gerbil *(JUR buhl)* is also called the *Mongolian jird.* Gerbils live in dry regions of Africa and Asia. The animal weighs about 3 ounces (85 grams) and measures about 8 inches (20 centimeters) long, including its tail. Gerbils eat plant bulbs, leaves, roots, seeds, and stems.

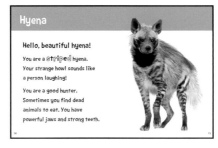

Pages 12-13 Hare
Jack rabbits are found in deserts and prairies in western North America. The antelope jack rabbit, the largest kind, weighs about 8 pounds (3.6 kilograms). It grows to nearly 27 inches (69 centimeters) long. Jack rabbits like to eat *succulents,* plants with thick, juicy leaves or stems.

Pages 14-15 Hyena
The striped hyena *(hy EE nuh)* lives in northern Africa and from Turkey to India in Asia. Striped hyenas measure about 3 feet (1 meter) from head to tail. They weigh from 55 to 100 pounds (25 to 45 kilograms). The hyena hunts animals for its food. It also eats the dead animals it finds.

Pages 16-17 Lizard
The Gila *(HEE luh)* monster lives primarily in the Sonoran Desert of the southwestern United States and northern Mexico. It usually grows about 19 inches (48 centimeters) long. It eats bird and reptile eggs and young mammals.

Pages 18-19 Owl
The burrowing owl lives in deserts and grasslands of the Americas. It grows about 9 inches (23 centimeters) long. Burrowing owls hunt mainly insects and rodents.

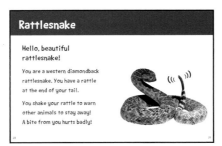

Pages 20-21 Rattlesnake
The western diamondback rattlesnake is found from Arkansas and Texas to California in the United States and in nearby Mexico. It grows 3 to 5 feet (1 to 1.5 meters) in length. It eats birds and small mammals. It will also occasionally feed on amphibians, reptiles, and other small animals.

Pages 22-23 Scorpion
The stripe-tailed scorpion (SKAWR pee uhn) lives mainly in the south-western United States. Adults grow up to 2 ½ inches (64 millimeters) in length. Scorpions eat insects and spiders.

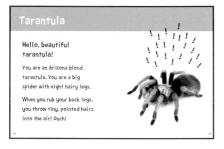

Pages 24-25 Tarantula
The Arizona blond tarantula (tuh RAN chuh luh) lives in the deserts of the southwestern United States and northern Mexico. The spider reaches about 3 to 5 inches (7.5 to 13 centimeters) in length. Females are larger than males. Arizona blond tarantulas feed primarily on large insects and other small animals.

Pages 26-27 Vulture
The griffon vulture (VUHL chuhr) lives in parts of southern Europe, northern and western Africa, the Middle East, and southern and central Asia. The griffon vulture is about 3 feet (1 meter) long with a wingspread of about 7 ½ to 9 feet (2.3 to 2.8 meters). It feeds mostly on the carcasses of dead animals.

Pages 28-29 Wren
The cactus wren (rehn) lives in dry regions of the southwestern United States and northern Mexico. It is the largest wren in North America, measuring 7 to 8 ¾ inches (18 to 22.2 centimeters) in length. Cactus wrens primarily eat insects (including ants, beetles, grasshoppers, and wasps) and occasional seeds and fruits.

Index